# Contents

# Publishing update

This guide was first published in 1994. This edition is a reprint with a revised format and further reading section (page 20), otherwise the text has not been altered. The section on further reading has been updated to include relevant advice published since 1994. Please note that all references to *Forestry Authority* should be read as *Forestry Commission*.

**Forestry Commission**

## Practice Guide

# The Management of Semi-natural Woodlands

## 2. Lowland Beech–Ash Woods

**Forestry Commission: Edinburgh**

First published in 1994 by the Forestry Commission
231 Corstorphine Road, Edinburgh EH12 7AT.

Reprinted 2003

Applications for reproduction of any part of this
Practice Guide should be addressed to:
HMSO, Licensing Division, St Clements House,
2–16 Colegate, Norwich NR3 1BQ.

ISBN 0 85538 581 2

FORESTRY COMMISSION (1994).
*The management of semi-natural woodlands:*
*2. Lowland beech–ash woods.*
Forestry Commission Practice Guide.
Forestry Commission, Edinburgh. i–iv + 1–28pp.

Keywords: ancient woodlands, biodiversity, lowland beech–ash
woods, native woodlands, nature conservation, semi-natural
woodlands, sustainable forest management.

Printed in the United Kingdom
on Robert Horne Hello.

FCPG002/PPD(KMA)/LTHPT-4000/MAR03

Enquiries relating to this publication should be addressed to:

Policy & Practice Division
Forestry Commission
231 Corstorphine Road
Edinburgh
EH12 7AT

Tel:  0131 334 0303
Fax: 0131 316 4344

## Acknowledgements

The compilation of this Guide was a team effort involving the following people. Dr George Peterken, acted as project adviser and drafted much of the text. Richard Britton and latterly Gordon Patterson were Project Leaders. John Clarke, Conservator Kent and East Sussex, and Graham Darrah undertook the initial research visits and prepared a report on which this Guide is based; they also commented on later drafts. Colin Tubbs, Barry Teasdale, Francis Rose and Tony Whitbread gave valuable comments and Alastair Rowan helped in various stages of the drafting. Alistair Scott and Graham Gill, provided additional editorial input. Many other organisations and individuals provided useful advice and comment at various stages.

# Introduction

Ancient semi-natural woodlands are a vital part of our heritage. They provide a range of habitats which support a rich diversity of plants and animals. Many woodland species depend entirely for their survival on the continued existence of these habitats. Ancient semi-natural woodlands form prominent features in many landscapes and collectively constitute a significant economic resource. They are all that remain of the original forests which covered most of Britain and now occupy only 1% of land area. Concern about the continuing loss of area and character of ancient woods contributed to the Government's decision to introduce the Broadleaves Policy in 1985.

The Broadleaves Policy aims to maintain and increase the broadleaved woodland by encouraging good management for a wide range of objectives and giving special attention to ancient semi-natural woodlands to maintain their special features. It has generally been very successful in encouraging the expansion and better management of broadleaved woodland and in preventing further losses of ancient semi-natural broadleaved woodland. However, there is a need for policy guidance to take more account of local and regional factors, especially for semi-natural woodlands which vary greatly in character in response to differences in climate, soils and history.

The management guidelines for the native pinewoods of the Scottish Highlands published by the Forestry Commission in 1989 have proved a successful example of guidance for a specific type of semi-natural woodland. We have now extended this approach into a comprehensive set of advisory guides on the management of ancient semi-natural woods throughout Britain. For this purpose, we recognise eight broad woodland types as described in the Appendix.

The advice is intended to help owners and managers to achieve the best practice which will secure the woodland's future. The guides describe the management most appropriate for each type of woodland. Devised by Forestry Commission staff working closely with

foresters and ecologists with special knowledge and experience of managing British semi-natural woodlands, they form a distillation of the best advice available.

Whilst these guides are aimed primarily at ancient semi-natural woodland, much of the advice in them will also be appropriate for other semi-natural woods which are of high conservation value, and for long-established planted woods which have developed some of the characteristics of ancient semi-natural woodland, notably where native trees were planted on ancient woodland sites.

The ecological value and character of ancient semi-natural woodland varies considerably. Some, notably in less accessible upland areas, owe much of their current value to a relatively low intensity of past management, although none have been totally unaffected by human influence. Others, especially in the lowlands, have developed a distinctively rich flora and fauna through a long history of consistent silvicultural management. Some have lost many of their special characteristics through various types of disturbance and many have been reduced in size so much that their survival is at risk. All are part of the nation's heritage, and deserve forms of management which recognise their different values. Some are designated as Sites of Special Scientific Interest. These may have specific management arrangements agreed with the conservation agencies, which are outside the scope of these booklets. The advice given here is aimed at encouraging forms of management which maintain and enhance the special characteristics of all ancient semi-natural woodland.

When grant aid is sought the Forestry Authority will compare management proposals with the advice contained in these booklets. Applicants are free to propose other forms of management for these woods, but must satisfy the Forestry Authority that their proposals will be effective in maintaining, and preferably enhancing, the special characteristics of the woodland. The advice given in these booklets is intended to create a flexible framework rather than a straight-jacket, so that woods and their owners can develop their individuality as much as possible without reducing options for future generations.

Sensitive management which takes account of the individual character and circumstances of woods, and also the particular objectives of owners, is essential if their values are to be successfully maintained.

The appropriate form of management will vary considerably. In some cases, particularly some upland and many wet woodlands the most suitable management will be to reduce grazing and browsing pressures from deer or stock to levels which will allow natural regeneration or expansion of the wood to happen. More intensive forms of management may harm the unique wildlife interest of some of these woods. Elsewhere, especially in lowland woods with a long history of management systems such as coppice with standards, more active forms of silviculture will be appropriate and often necessary to conserve their character and wildlife as well as their value as an economic resource.

One thing which is certain is that positive management will be needed if we are to continue recent progress in halting the decline of our semi-natural woods and to restore them to a healthy condition to hand on to our successors as vital parts of our heritage.

*Bird's nest orchid*

# Management principles for semi-natural and native woodlands

**Semi-natural woods** are composed of locally native trees and shrubs which derive from natural regeneration or coppicing rather than planting. Because of their natural features and appearance, semi-natural woods are valuable for nature conservation and in the landscape, and many are important for recreation and for historical and cultural interest.

Management should aim to maintain and enhance these values in harmony with securing other benefits, including wood products.

**Ancient semi-natural woodlands are of special value** because of their long, continuous history. They are the nearest we have to our original natural woodland and include remnants of the post-glacial forest which have never been cleared. They are irreplaceable assets which support many rare plants and animals and make a vital contribution to conserving biodiversity. They also contain a wealth of evidence of our past. Many have been greatly modified in structure and composition by centuries of management, whilst retaining many natural features. Some are threatened by neglect in the face of pressures such as fragmentation and overgrazing. The Forestry Authority encourages management which seeks to maintain or restore their special characteristics, including their natural diversity of species and habitats, aesthetic and cultural values and genetic integrity, whilst taking appropriate opportunities for wood production for a range of markets.

**Management proposals should be geared to sensitive and low-key methods which are suited to the natural dynamics of these woodlands. Natural regeneration will be preferred to planting wherever practicable.** More detailed guidance is given in the guide for each woodland type.

**Other semi-natural woodlands,** which have developed from natural colonisation of open ground sometime within the last few centuries, are also normally of high environmental value, particularly in the uplands, although they are not usually so valuable as ancient semi-natural woodlands because of their shorter history.

**Appropriate management will vary according to the relative importance of these woodlands. For some, for example many long-established upland woods, management should be similar to that for ancient woods, whilst in woods of lower value a greater range of silvicultural options will be acceptable.**

**Planted woods of native species** may often acquire some of the characteristics of semi-natural woodland, especially where they are on **ancient woodland sites,** where plants and animals have survived from the former semi-natural wood. The development of a varied structure and composition, including diverse native tree, shrub and field layer vegetation and the use of locally native species and genotypes for planted trees, can also increase the naturalness of native plantations.

Where planted native woods have developed a high conservation value in these ways **management should be similar to that for semi-natural woods, but generally a wider range of silvicultural systems, including a greater emphasis on planting instead of natural regeneration, will be permitted under the grant aid and felling regulations.**

**New native woodlands,** which are designed and managed from the start to develop a natural character, can help to offset some of the past losses of native woodland and will in time acquire a high environmental value, although they should not be seen as substitutes for any remaining semi-natural woodland.

**The Forestry Authority will encourage by grant-aid the creation of new native woodlands on open land by natural colonisation or planting, where species composition and site are suitably matched, especially on areas close to existing semi-natural woods.** Further guidance can be obtained in Bulletin 112, published by the Forestry Authority.

# What are lowland beech–ash woods?

*Ash*

This guide deals mainly with management of the ancient semi-natural beech–ash woods of southern England and south-east Wales, but it also includes guidance on the yew woods which are sometimes associated with them. Both are concentrated on base-rich soils: rendzinas and brown earth soils developed over chalk and limestones and other alkaline or mildly acid clays and loams. They occur in well-defined groups on the South Downs, North Downs, Chilterns, Cotswolds, lower Wye Valley and the Carboniferous limestones of South Wales. There are estimated to be 10 000–15 000 hectares of ancient semi-natural woodlands of this type.

A typical example would be a tall, beech-dominated woodland running up a steep, chalkland scarp over the ridge and onto the heavier soils of the plateau. Within such woods ash regenerates well in gaps and can form ashwoods with little or no beech. Both ends of this range are covered in this guide.

The National Vegetation Classification (Rodwell 1991[1]) recognises two types of beech–ash woodland and separates the yew woods into a third type. A characteristic feature of all three types is the dominance of a few tree species. Indeed, it is common for more than 90% of the trees in a beech–ash wood to be beech, and the dominance of yew in yew woods is often so complete that few other trees and shrubs grow with it.

## Beech–dog's mercury woodland (W12)

This is the characteristic beech–ash woodland of freely-drained calcareous soils on sloping sites. The steepest examples form 'hangers' on the chalk scarps and cling to limestone bluffs in the Wye Gorge. Less extreme examples develop in coombes and on the lower slopes of re-entrant valleys. Beech is characteristically accompanied by ash, gean, field maple, wych elm, pedunculate oak, sessile oak and locally small-leaved and large-leaved limes. Where the beech is not absolutely dominant and the soil is shallow, a diverse underwood of yew, holly,

whitebeam and other shrubs develops. In a few sites the shrub layer includes native populations of box. On the deeper soils, hazel and hawthorn appear. Sycamore is well-established in many woods. As its name indicates, dog's mercury commonly carpets the ground, with sanicle, ivy, wild arum, sweet woodruff and wood avens. On the moister examples, primrose, yellow archangel, wood anemone are common.

## Beech–bramble woodland (W14)

This is the characteristic form of beech woodland growing on the clays and clay loams of the chalkland plateaus and other superficial deposits. Such soils are mildly acid, base-poor and often poorly-drained, but the beech grows taller here than in the previous type. Ash is far less abundant, but pedunculate oak is common, with gean, birch and naturalised sycamore. The beech in the overstorey is often so abundant and vigorous that shrubs are rare, but most examples have a scatter of holly, hawthorn, hazel, yew and goat willow. Deep thickets of bramble form when the canopy is broken or loses vigour. Other common ground flora associates include bluebell, wood sorrel, male fern, tufted hair-grass, creeping soft-grass and wood spurge. Beech–bramble woodland often grades into mixtures of oak, hazel and ash on poorly-drained, heavy soils.

## Yew woodland (W13)

Yew often forms a dense underwood in beechwoods on the steepest and driest slopes, but it also forms a distinctive woodland type on similar sites in the absence of beech, especially on very dry, south-facing chalk slopes and the bottoms of dry valleys of the North and South Downs. These are perhaps the least diverse of all British woodlands. Yew is often so dominant that only a scatter of hazel, whitebeam or ash may be present. The ground vegetation, if not entirely absent, is rarely more than a thin scatter of dog's mercury, wild arum, violets and wild strawberry. Yew woods also occur sparingly in northern and western Britain.

# History and traditional management

After the last ice-age, beech was slow to return to Britain. In fact, it had probably not reached its climatic limits before the original woodlands were mostly cleared. Thus, although it is strictly native only in southern England and south Wales, it can spread vigorously after introduction to woodlands further north and west, to which, given time, it might have penetrated naturally. Within its native range beech rose to dominance in woods which were disturbed by wood cutting and pasturage. Most beech–ash woods were managed either as coppice-with-standards or as wood-pasture in the medieval period. Under the former regime, beech was merely one species within mixed coppice growing below oak standards. Within the latter, beech and oak assumed greater prominence, partly because they were pollarded and thereby outlived other species. In the 18th and 19th centuries, however, these systems were largely replaced by high forest beechwoods, many of which were maintained by selective fellings for furniture making. Selection in favour of beech, combined with the heavy shade cast by it, converted these hitherto mixed woods containing some beech to woodland absolutely dominated by beech.

Many of the beech–ash high forest woods regenerated 150–200 years ago. Many have been felled in recent decades, and in those which have not, mature trees have often died or have been blown over, leaving gaps in the canopy. In 1987 and 1990, storms took a particularly heavy toll, levelling some of the most exposed stands. The gaps have been colonised by ash, sycamore, hazel and other shrubs, thereby diversifying the woods.

Although most beech–ash woods now have a high forest structure, coppice forms survive locally in the Cotswolds and lower Wye valley. In the Chilterns, some woods on Poors' Allotments take the form of beech coppice. Wood-pastures have virtually vanished from this woodland type.

The conversion from traditional forms of management to high forest was achieved in many woods by planting. Ancient Scots pine,

European larch and Norway spruce still survive in some woods from the initial mixed plantings. At the same time, some unwooded ground was also planted, and from these plantings mature beech woods have grown which are difficult to distinguish from the beechwoods on ancient woodland sites. Indeed, because they often grow so close to the ancient woods, they have been colonised by many of the characteristic woodland plants and animals. Some retain relict patches of the former chalk grassland.

Most yew woods, unlike most of the beech woods, are secondary. They developed by natural colonisation of chalk grassland amongst a variety of shrub species, such as juniper, dogwood, rose. In due course, the other shrubs were outgrown and outlasted by the yew, which has assumed absolute dominance. In some instances, a scatter of ash, oak or beech established themselves at the same time as the yew and have grown fast enough to develop a patchy overstorey above the yew.

*Beech*

# Values

*Red helleborine*

## Landscape

Beech–ash woods are prominent features in the landscape, because they are tall, occupy conspicuous positions and generally occur in groups. The Chilterns, central Cotswold scarp and parts of the Downs owe much of their beauty to the beechwoods. The silvery-grey trunks of mature beech in winter and the fresh green leaves and carpets of bluebells of early May are amongst the chief glories of the lowland landscape.

## Historical and cultural

The beech–ash woods of the chalk and limestone slopes are permeated by old tracks, lanes and ancient hollow-ways, which were used both to gain access to ancient grazings on the summits and slopes and to extract timber and firewood. They are usually narrow and prone to damage by forest and farm machinery.

These lanes are often lined by ancient coppice stools of beech, ash and maple, relicts of the hedges which bounded the woods before they grew to high forest. Rarer species, such as sessile oak, whitebeam and lime are also found, a reminder of the mixtures that once characterised the coppices. The only native small-leaved lime in the Chilterns is in such a place. In the South Downs, several examples of the very rare large-leaved lime have recently been found in ancient woodland hedges.

Some beech–ash woods have developed in land which was farmed or inhabited in early medieval and earlier times. Such woods may be protecting important archaeological features.

## Wildlife conservation

The richest assemblages tend to occur in beech–dog's mercury woodland, particularly on the drier sites where mercury is less vigorous. Here rare orchids, such as lady orchid, white helleborine, green helleborine, narrow-lipped helleborine and, exceptionally, the red helleborine grow, dependent on mycorrhizal associations. Bird's-nest orchid, yellow bird's nest and the exceptionally rare ghost orchid grow saprophytically, totally dependent on fungal associates. Another group of rare plants is associated with disturbed ground and marginal scrub, including green hound's tongue, military orchid and Tintern spurge. Commoner species with a wider distribution include early purple orchid, hairy violet, herb paris, plough-man's spikenard, aquilegia and twayblade.

Amongst the commoner and widespread species are several woodland grasses, such as wood false brome, wood melick, hairy brome and bearded couch-grass. The beech–bramble type often has wood millet and creeping soft grass. On the whole, the beech–bramble woods contain fewer species, but include attractive common species such as honeysuckle, sweet woodruff and wood spurge, and the local butcher's broom and violet helleborine.

The beech–dog's mercury type includes several locations for rare native trees and shrubs. The large-leaved lime has already been mentioned and the few native populations of box at Box Hill, Norbury Park, Chequers and a few other places are well known, but there are also some endemic whitebeams in the Wye Gorge beech–woods and mezereon occurs in a few sites.

## Recreation

Most beech–ash woods lie in the Home Counties or in famously attractive countryside. They are permeated by footpaths and bridleways affording wide view over lowland countryside. Small car parks, picnic sites and signposted long-distance paths have further opened them up to visitors. Some beech–ash woods form part of well-loved and heavily used beauty spots.

## Game and livestock

Although many woods were grazed in the past and some have grown up on old pastures, most beech–ash woods are not used for pasturage.

Indeed, many contain yew, which is poisonous to grazing animals. Downland pastures sometimes border beech–ash woods and admit animals to the woods.

Beech-dominated woodlands with a sparse underwood have little value for game-birds.

## Wood production

Beech–ash woods have yielded valuable oak timber when they were managed as coppice-with-standards and more recently have supplied the furniture trade and many other markets with beech timber. The beech–bramble type is potentially productive, but the beech–dog's mercury type is less vigorous and more vulnerable to drought. Today, these woods could yield moderate-quality beech, oak, ash, cherry and perhaps sycamore, and some specialist timbers, notably yew. These include major hardwood species well capable of substituting for tropical hardwoods.

*Mezereon*

# Policy aims

The aims of policy are to encourage appropriate management of semi-natural lowland beech–ash and yew woods so as to:

- **Maintain and wherever suitable restore the natural ecological diversity;**

- **Maintain and where appropriate improve their aesthetic value.**

These two aims should be applied in every case. In the great majority of woods they should be compatible with each other but where conflicts do occur the first should tend to take priority over the second because of the national importance of ancient semi-natural woodland for nature conservation. However, each wood should be assessed according to its importance in the landscape and for nature conservation.

- **Maintain the genetic integrity of populations of native species, so far as is practicable.**

This aim is relevant for semi-natural woodlands where the genetic integrity of native tree and shrub populations has not been seriously compromised by past introductions of non-native stock within or close to the woodland.

- **Take appropriate opportunities to produce utilisable wood.**

The production of utilisable wood, including timber, is not an obligatory aim for every woodland. It is possible to achieve all the other policy aims without it, and indeed in a minority of woods where minimal intervention is an appropriate philosophy, wood production may not be desirable. However, for many owners, securing an adequate income from their woodlands is essential in ensuring the continuity of management necessary to achieve these aims. Improving timber values, and hence the financial viability of the woodland, in ways compatible with other aims, is therefore a general strategy which the Forestry Authority encourages.

Most semi-natural lowland beech–ash and yew woodlands are capable of yielding high quality timber products which, with good management as suggested in this guide, can be harvested in ways which are compatible with achieving the other policy aims.

- **Enlarge the woods where possible.**

Expansion of ancient semi-natural woodlands is very often desirable especially for small woods to secure their long-term future.

Each wood is unique in its characteristics and its relationship to the surrounding landscape. Although many beech–ash woods have become fairly uniform, due to past encouragement of beech monocultures, most encompass significant small-scale variety of site conditions. Within practicable limits, the aim should be to reflect this inherent diversity in future management.

# Application of this guide

This guide should be applied to all ancient semi-natural lowland beech–ash woods and yew woods of this type managed under the Woodland Grant Scheme. They will normally qualify for the special rate of management grant where work is done to improve or maintain the special environmental value of the wood. It will also apply to Felling Licence applications, to management under other grant schemes and to woodlands in the management of Forest Enterprise.

Semi-natural lowland beech–ash and yew woodlands of recent origin are usually less valuable than ancient ones for nature conservation, so it is usually appropriate for management to place a relatively greater emphasis on timber production in recent woods, but otherwise much of this guide can be used.

Much of the advice in this guide can also be applied to ancient woodlands which have been converted to broadleaved or mixed plantations. The nature conservation value of these woods is generally less than that of ancient semi-natural woods, so it is usually legitimate to place a greater emphasis on timber production. In ancient woods which have been converted to conifer plantations, but which have retained some nature conservation value, there may be opportunities to restore semi-natural lowland beech–ash and yew woodlands to at least part of the wood by including appropriate native trees and shrubs in the next rotation.

Old planted woods of native species on sites which had not previously been wooded sometimes acquire conservation values nearly as high as those of ancient semi-natural woodland. Again much of this guide can be applied in these cases.

Where the woodland is designated as a Site of Special Scientific Interest (SSSI) guidance must be sought from English Nature or the Countryside Council for Wales, before carrying out any operation or change of management. Any other legal constraint on management, such as a Tree Preservation Order or a Scheduled Ancient Monument, must of course be respected.

# The management plan

For any woodland to receive grant aid from the Forestry Authority, management objectives and a programme of work must be agreed for a five year period.

In the case of semi-natural woods, especially the larger and more complex ones, it will be helpful to prepare a separate management plan, which can be used for reference when the detailed proposals are revised every five years on grant applications. The management plan should contain an assessment of the woodland, including any special characteristics, a statement of objects of management and their priorities and a long-term strategy setting out the desired future condition of the wood and how it is proposed to achieve it. This will be of great value for semi-natural woods where management should be particularly sensitive to the individual values and character of each woodland. The management plan should be brief and succinct; long descriptive essays are not likely to be read.

Here is a checklist of some of the factors to be included where relevant:

## Description

- Name, location.

- Areas, with sub-divisions if these clarify management proposals.

- Historical aspects, including past management.

- Tree and shrub species, notably dominant trees and abundant underwood shrubs.

- Age class distribution of trees; stocking; composition and condition of any natural regeneration.

- Ground flora; dominant species and any unusual species.

- Fauna, especially any rare, unusual, attractive or notable species.

- Conspicuousness in the landscape.

- Cultural features.

- Statutory designations.

- Constraints.

- Existing public access and planned future access.

The description should be a brief summary of the main features, ideally based upon survey information.

Local Forestry Authority officers may be able to advise on sources of specialist advice and survey information.

## Evaluation

Itemise any special values, e.g. prominent in landscape, rare species, natural features, historical associations, quality timber potential. Careful assessment of the values of the wood will help to generate suitable management objectives.

## Objects of management

All the policy aims must be respected, although as explained earlier not all are relevant to every wood. The owner may have additional objects of management for a wood. The owner should express the particular policy aims for the wood, giving details of management objectives and indicating priorities. Owners may find it helpful to discuss their objectives with local Forestry Authority staff.

## Management proposals

A long-term strategy should be stated, which specifies any changes in composition envisaged, the overall woodland structure which is sought and any silvicultural systems to be used. It would be helpful to state the reasons for adopting this strategy. The timescale may be many decades or more than a century. A five year summary work plan should be proposed, itemising the areas to be worked and the main operations to be carried out in the next five years.

## Monitoring

A vital stage, often omitted, is the monitoring and review of management. Has it delivered the desired results? An ideal review point is the revision of a grant scheme or plan of operations every five years. Monitoring requires that some record be made of what the wood was like at the start of the period, the work done and how the wood responded. Experience demonstrates that, even in small and well-known areas, memory seldom provides the level of detail and accuracy required. Monitoring should be targeted to assessing how well the objectives of management are being achieved. This may mean, for example, assessing the success of natural regeneration or changes in woodland structure and species composition. Where rare habitats or species are present their progress may also be monitored in response to woodland management.

Simple techniques such as fixed-point photography can be used by non-specialists and provide valuable information over the years. Amateur naturalists as well as professional ecologists may be able to help with monitoring the wildlife of woods.

Some sources of advice on monitoring are listed in Further Reading and Forestry Authority staff may also be able to advise on what is needed for individual woods.

*Field maple*

# Operational guidelines

## General principles

The policy aims for beech–ash woods lead to general principles for management:

- **Maintain semi-natural woodland types.**

Management should be based on growing species native to the site and appropriate to the pattern of soils within the site. Existing abundant species should remain a significant component.

- **Improve diversity of structure.**

A range of age classes within each site is preferred to the single age class which is frequently encountered.

- **Increase diversity of species, where appropriate.**

Many beech–ash woods are dominated by beech, due to past treatments.

- **Maintain diversity of habitat.**

A diverse structure and mixture of species improves habitat diversity, but open space is also extremely important. It can be temporary (recently cut areas) or permanent (e.g. rides).

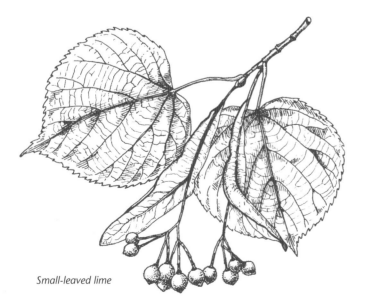

*Small-leaved lime*

- **Maintain a mature habitat.**

This can be achieved by retaining old, dead or dying trees either standing or fallen, and by increasing rotation lengths.

- **Minimise rates of change.**

Wildlife takes time to adjust, so change should not be too drastic. This applies both to the scale and sequence of felling, and the layout of the wood.

- **Use low-key establishment techniques.**

Aggressive working methods should be avoided. The general rule should be to do the minimum necessary to ensure adequate establishment and growth.

## The need for management

Although a few beech–ash woods within nature reserves may legitimately be left unmanaged indefinitely for scientific purposes, most woods of this type are better managed than neglected. This is obviously true if timber production is an aim, but it is also true for landscape and nature conservation. Regularly treated woods can have a mixed age-structure, retain open-space habitats and will remain less vulnerable to catastrophic disturbances than unmanaged woods. Many stands of 19th century origin are now urgently in need of regeneration.

## Silvicultural systems

### High forest
Beech–ash woods are particularly well suited to high forest systems worked by small-scale fellings. Beech bears shade and grows best as a maiden tree, and most of the associated trees bear moderate levels of shade. Coppice, however, is equally appropriate in woods of mixed composition and a recent history of coppicing.

Most beech–ash woods should be managed as uneven-aged high forest with a pattern of small groups. Groups should normally vary in size between 0.2–0.5 ha, with a width of around 1.5–2 times the top height of the stand, but smaller groups not larger than the space occupied by one or two mature trees are quite practicable for the shade-bearing trees. This produces a structure similar to that of natural beech woodlands, which regenerate mainly in small gaps. It creates structural diversity and a range of size classes, even in small woodlands. Given the ability of ash, cherry, sycamore, maple, hornbeam and lime to grow in moderate shade, it also permits a variety of species to co-exist.

The treatment should be adapted to local circumstances. In woods of less than 5 ha, especially if access is difficult, 'little and often' may be less practicable than longer intervals between fellings with somewhat larger regeneration groups.

The treatment should also be adapted to suit the species present, Shade-bearers, notably beech with ash, and sycamore where it is to be retained in the mixture, can be grown on a true selection system. Where light-demanding species, notably oak, are present and desired for timber, larger groups exceeding 0.5 ha or a shelterwood system will be desirable. Ash and cherry grow well within both scales of working, but the proportion of these species is generally greater with larger groups. Whereas beech grows on a 100–120 year rotation, ash and cherry do better at 60–80 years. Always encourage a dense understorey, thereby creating a more varied woodland structure of great benefit to wildlife and ensuring that timber stems remain clean.

## Coppice

Coppicing is recommended as a component of smaller woods and those woods which were coppiced within the last 50 years or so, providing browsing by deer can be controlled. Coppicing maintains the short cycle of light and shade to which the wildlife of most lowland ancient woods is adapted. It creates great habitat diversity and numerous edge habitats. It enables ride grassland to be maintained and preserves mixtures of trees and shrubs that have often remained stable for centuries.

Coppice is particularly appropriate for stands rich in ash, lime or hazel. Coppice-with-standards will produce the greatest habitat diversity and creates an opportunity to grow large oak, ash, cherry or lime quickly. Group planting of timber trees produces an intermediate condition between coppice and high forest which combines the value of both.

Most beech–ash woods suitable for coppicing are found in the Cotswolds and further west, where lime, wych elm, hazel and many other species grow in rich mixtures. When coppiced these produce some of the richest displays of woodland flowers in Britain.

## Woodland pasturage

Beech–ash woods are sometimes intermixed with long-established, herb-rich pastures, especially on chalk slopes and limestone hills. These habitat mixtures are usually the richest wildlife locations in the area, and should be maintained by regular grazing, even if access to woodland is unavoidable and the treatment of woodland has to be modified.

In the few surviving examples of parkland beech–ash woods, it is important to keep existing trees whilst planting a scatter of the same species in the open spaces.

## Harvesting

As the size of the groups decreases, so the felling skills required increase. In addition to the potential damage to standing trees, felling can damage groups of saplings already growing in earlier felled patches.

The heavy machinery used during felling and extraction can damage soil structure and archaeological features. The thin layer of litter, rich in important mycorrhizal fungi, is particularly vulnerable to erosion on disturbance and exposure to sun and rain. The damage to the woodland ecosystem would be most severe and longest-lasting on the steep chalkland slopes where many beech–ash woods are situated.

On the deeper, richer soils at the base of slopes and on the heavier clays of the beech–bramble type, prolonged use of heavy machinery can lead to soil compaction and localised waterlogging. Light disturbance and scarification benefits ground vegetation and natural regeneration, but heavy disturbance can lead to difficult weed problems with tufted hairgrass and rushes. Wherever possible, heavy machinery should be kept to existing tracks and rides. Operators should avoid crossing watercourses and other wet areas, banks, ditches and other archaeological features and avoid working when soils are waterlogged.

## Retained old trees and deadwood

Many woodland wildlife species depend on large, old trees, standing dead wood and large fallen trunks and limbs. Beech–ash woods, however, rarely contain truly ancient specimens and usually possess only limited amounts of dead wood. Nevertheless, the trunks of large trees are potentially rich habitats for lichens, and large fallen trunks or limbs provide habitats for fungi, insects and other woodland fauna.

Management should aim to maintain and increase the number of large, old trees and the quantity of dead wood. Large trees can be achieved by allowing some groups of trees to grow longer than might be commercially desirable, especially groups of long-lived species (oak, beech) which occupy windfirm sites. Particular mature trees may already be known to be important (e.g. as bat roosts, or as habitats for rare fungi). These should be retained and eventual replacements developed by retaining trees at the edges of compartments and in inaccessible corners.

Dead wood can be provided by leaving individual windblown trees where they lie, subject to access, safety and marketing objectives. This is especially appropriate for fallen trees in difficult corners, along streamsides and on margins.

In coppice woods, old stools can be retained by cutting above the level of the last cut. Stub trees and pollards should be maintained by

periodic cutting, including trees growing on woodland margins.

## Methods of regeneration

### Natural regeneration
Natural regeneration is preferred to planting. It maintains the natural distribution of tree species in relation to site conditions, allows a shrub component to grow with the trees, maintains local genotypes, and usually results in mixed stands of diverse structure. Beech, ash, birch and yew regenerate well on the drier sites. Beech produces good or very heavy mast crops irregularly with a long-term average of one year in three. On deeper, moister soils, ash and sycamore are likely to be more prolific.

Advance regeneration of beech, ash, field maple, sycamore and yew is frequently established below small gaps and light-canopied trees in beech–ash woods. Wherever possible it should be accepted except perhaps in the case of sycamore (see below). Felling and regeneration groups should ideally be created by enlarging the openings around patches of advance regeneration.

Where stands contain little advance regeneration, felling should be timed and designed carefully to give the best chance of obtaining the desired amount and composition of subsequent natural regeneration. Larger openings provide greater opportunities for light-demanding species, such as birch and oak, and provide good growing conditions for other species. Smaller openings generate groups of regeneration with mainly beech, ash, sycamore and yew. Dense bramble growth may be encouraged in the larger openings; beech seedlings find it difficult to penetrate this and may be killed by mildew. Beech–ash woods often have a nearly-invisible scatter of very small 1–3 year old seedlings, which, if they survive felling and extraction, can grown through bramble. Once a persistent bramble thicket is established, natural regeneration can be indefinitely postponed.

### Planting
Planting may be necessary to enrich natural regeneration or to fill blanks, but on thin-

soiled, drought-prone sites there is a high risk of failure. Enrichment with locally native species which are absent or inadequately represented in natural regeneration increases diversity and adds to the silvicultural options at a later stage. Any enrichment planting should normally be done within than 3 years of felling. Planting will often be necessary to achieve high densities if owners wish to produce oak timber of good quality, but will rarely be necessary for ash. Where timber production is less important a longer period may be allowed for natural regeneration to fill gaps with irregular mixtures.

Planting can be done with individual plants or by groups, distributed in an irregular manner across the site. Individual planted groups should be large enough to generate at least one final crop tree. Planting a variety of species in each group provides safeguards against failure and options for mid-rotation treatment. If tree shelters are to be used, the cost should be weighed against future benefits. Single trees planted in accessible spots may be the simplest way of establishing a broadleaved crop. Shelters help during weeding by making saplings visible.

Where 'nurse' species are required to improve the early growth and form of broadleaved timber species, they should themselves be broadleaved, and could take the form of coppice regrowth or natural seedlings. Conifer 'nurses' will rarely be appropriate in ancient semi-natural woodlands of this type, because they tend to deplete the diversity of naturally regenerating native trees and shrubs, the ground vegetation and associated animals, due to their shade and litter.

Beech and oak are covered by the Forest Reproductive Materials regulations so that planting stock should originate from a registered seed source, but small amounts of seed can be sold from unregistered sources (sufficient for a thousand plants or less) if it is to be used for conservation rather than forestry purposes.

Local sources are generally preferable and are particularly important in stands where there is little evidence of past planting such as old coppice woods.

## Coppicing

Coppice rotations depend on species, growth rates and markets for produce. Ecologically, the need is to cut some coppice every few years to maintain open spaces and young growth as a permanent feature somewhere in the wood. Rotations longer than 30 years produce much more saleable products but are too long to secure the best conservation benefits. Nevertheless, shorter rotations are not recommended, unless there are markets for the produce or large identifiable benefits for conservation.

Coppiced woods regenerate vigorously as a mixture of stool sprouts and new regeneration. Special measures are rarely required to achieve good regeneration, but planting of a few oaks will safeguard against poor natural regeneration of this valuable timber species. Beech coppice sprouts more vigorously if one stem is retained on each stool. Protection of coppice shrubs against deer will often be vital.

## Site preparation

Beech–ash woods are usually well drained, but damp areas can occur behind banks, in gulleys and on heavier plateau soils. Drainage of these patches is undesirable: wet areas and temporary puddles are essential elements of habitat diversity on which many woodland species depend.

Limited disturbance of freely drained mineral soil is often beneficial on flat ground and gentle slopes. It is a substitute for the natural soil turnover which occurs when large trees are blown over. It stimulates regeneration by burying fruits (such as acorns) which might otherwise be eaten, re-activating dormant seed and by releasing nutrients. Light screefing after a heavy seed fall is especially effective.

## Weeding

Ground vegetation consists of native plants and provides a substrate for woodland fauna, so weeding should be minimised. Certain stand treatments on heavier soils give rise to growths of bramble, bracken or coarse grasses which inhibit regeneration and growth. Weeding is normally required for the first 3–4 years in

*Wood melick*

order to ensure that transplants are not smothered. Herbicides should be used mainly for grassy vegetation and should normally be spot applications limited to a spot of one metre diameter around the planted trees. Hand-cutting is preferable for wildlife conservation where grasses are not dominant in the ground vegetation, especially if it can be delayed until late June. Alternatively where beech is the main seedling species hand-cutting in February is suitable when the retained dead leaves make seedlings easy to see.

## Tending and thinning

Thinning is necessary to grow good timber, but it can significantly influence the conservation value of a wood. All the species in a natural mixture should be retained as late into the rotation as possible, and preferably into the final crop. Final thinnings can be

designed to achieve advance regeneration. Heavy and early thinning will enable a shrub layer to persist or develop, retain a vigorous ground vegetation and allow shade-tolerant trees to form a productive underwood. Patches with different intensities of thinning will allow some structural diversity into a wood which might otherwise be uniform. Thinning also provides an opportunity to bring in some early income.

In naturally-regenerated stands respacing should be done about year 15, though beech can be left somewhat longer without detriment. Beech will continue to regenerate into ash groups for up to 15 year after initial establishment, slowly outgrowing the surrounding ash. If thinning is postponed, beech tend to grow with flat tops which cannot subsequently grow into tall, straight stems. The overwood must be removed while the regeneration is still supple enough to withstand extraction damage. Groups in beech–ash woods should normally be thinned first after 30–40 years and last at about 80–90 years, or some 20 years before final crop trees are felled. Stems should be selected for vigour, good form and potential timber value, but the aim should be to maintain a mixture of species in the stand throughout the rotation. Beech and oak may be favoured more strongly in the final thinning but other species should still be retained to some extent.

Long-neglected beech stands can be improved by thinning at all ages. This provides an alternative to clear felling when rehabilitating a wood.

Coppice does not require thinning but decisions must be taken when cutting about which poles to retain as standards. Beech is not recommended because its heavy shade damages the underwood. Oak is preferred, both for timber value and as habitat. Ideally, a few individuals of other species should also be retained as standards.

## Exotic species

Sycamore commonly colonises beech–ash woods, especially on deeper soils, and in many woods it has been planted. Where it is well-established, sycamore may be retained but as a small part of the mixture, not as a monoculture. If it is present in only small quantities, say under 10%, then it should be removed from ancient semi-natural woods. Excessive sycamores should be removed in stages, choosing the moment which will maximise returns. It can be used as a nurse in woods where it is already strongly present, provided no native species is available and suitable. Sycamore and other non-native trees should not be introduced into ancient semi-natural woods where they are not already present.

## Nutrition

Beech growing on thin, dry soils suffer from lime chlorosis, but no practicable treatment is available. Nitrogen applications can damage tree roots and will generate vigorous weed competition.

## Grazing and browsing

Low intensity grazing and browsing is a natural feature of woodlands which helps to maintain diversity in composition and structure. However deer, rabbits and hares can cause serious damage to young trees and coppice shoots. Ideally, they should be controlled at low population levels, combined with protection for seedlings and saplings if and when damage becomes significant. The most effective form of protection is by fencing, tree guards or shelters. Shelters are usually cheaper than fencing for irregular areas and small groups. They also help during weeding by making protected trees – both planted and naturally regenerated – more visible.

## Grey squirrel control

Grey squirrels can cause serious bark-stripping damage to many trees between about 10 and 40 years of age, particularly to beech, sycamore and to a lesser extent oak.

Control methods are described in FC Research Information Notes 180[2], 191[3] and 232[4]. The most effective method is the use of Warfarin bait in hoppers which are designed to prevent non-target animals from entering and being poisoned.

Poison cannot legally be used for grey squirrel control in some counties in England and Wales where red squirrels are present. In these areas cage-trapping and spring-trapping are the only suitable methods.

## Open ground

Open areas in semi-natural woodlands provide exceptionally important habitats. In beech–ash woodlands rides often support many of the herbs which are characteristic of chalk and limestone grassland. On their margins they have concentrations of shrubs and small trees, such as dogwood, whitebeam, sallow and hazel. Together with the adjacent woodland, they form a mixture of habitats which generate concentrations of wildlife. Maintaining these open and edge habitats is an important reason why woodland nature conservation generally requires management, not neglect. Cutting will usually be necessary. Rides and roadside can be improved by judicious widening or scalloping, and by creating large open areas at junctions.

Beech–ash woods often contain enclaves of long-established chalk and limestone grassland, especially on steeper slopes. These should not be planted or allowed to grow into mature woodland. Scrub encroaching from the margins should be cut back every 5–10 years.

## Minimum intervention areas

Whilst wildlife generally benefits from management in accordance with this guide, it is not necessary for environmental gains for every part of all woodlands to be actively managed. Awkward or remote corners, steep-sided streamsides, rock outcrops and sites on steep slopes with very shallow and drought-prone soils can be left completely unmanaged to grow large trees and build up accumulations of dead wood, which would provide habitats for specialised and now often rare species. Where such non-intervention patches are explicitly maintained within the management plan the need for retained old trees elsewhere in the wood may be correspondingly reduced.

## Yew woodland

Pure yew woodlands grow in a few places on very dry sites. These developed by colonising grassland and it is uncertain whether they can be successfully regenerated as yew woods. On cutting they may regenerate more as ash or birch woods, with yew as a scattered underwood. Management of these limited areas should be restricted to very occasional harvesting of yews or box coppice along with more active management to maintain the chalk grassland glades within the wood.

Yew-rich beech–ash woods are also characteristic of the driest sites. Here yew develops as an underwood beneath the maturing broadleaf canopy. Felling the overstorey can promote rapid growth in the yew but little regeneration of broadleaves. If the wood as a whole is being treated on a group system, it is recommended that the yew be retained to commercial maturity. Broad-leaves will regenerate naturally when this is cut.

*Whitebeam*

# Expanding lowland beech–ash woods

Expansion should be encouraged where
adjacent ground is suitable but not onto
valuable chalk grassland habitats which should
be conserved as such.

Where expansion is desirable it should
preferably be by natural colonisation, with
planting perhaps used to increase the stocking
of timber species if required.

Further advice can be obtained in Forestry
Commission Bulletin 112[5].

# References

1.  RODWELL, J. S. (Ed) (1991). British plant communities. Volume 1, *Woodlands and scrub*. Cambridge University Press.

2.  FORESTRY COMMISSION (1990). *Grey squirrel damage control with Warfarin*. Forestry Commission Research Information Note 180. Forestry Commission, Edinburgh.

3.  FORESTRY COMMISSION (1990). *Grey squirrels and the law*. Forestry Commission Research Information Note 191. Forestry Commission, Edinburgh.

4.  FORESTRY COMMISSION (1993). Grey squirrel control using modified hoppers. Forestry Commission Research Information Note 232. Forestry Commission, Edinburgh.

5.  FORESTRY COMMISSION (1994). *Creating new native woodlands*. Forestry Commission Bulletin 112. HMSO, London.

6.  PETERKEN, G. F. (1993). *Woodland conservation and management* (2nd edition). Chapman and Hall, London.

# Useful sources of information

## Forestry Commission publications

The UK Forestry Standard (1998).

### Guidelines
Forest nature conservation (1990).
Forest recreation (1992).
Lowland landscape design (1992).
Community woodland design (1992).
Forest landscape design (2nd edition) (1994).
Forests and archaeology (1995).
Forests and soil conservation (1998).
Forests and water (3rd edition + amendments) (2000).

### Guideline Note
1 Forests and peatland habitats (2000).

### Practice Guide
Restoration of native woodland on ancient woodland sites (2003).

### Practice Notes
4 Controlling grey squirrel damage to woodlands (2003).
6 Managing deer in the countryside (1999).
8 Using local stock for planting native trees and shrubs (1999).

### Bulletins
62 Silviculture of broadleaved woodland (1984).
73 Rhododendron ponticum as a forest weed (1987).
78 Natural regeneration of broadleaves (1988).
91 The timbers of farm woodland trees (1990).
105 Roe deer biology and management (1992).
106 Woodland management for pheasants (1992).
108 Monitoring vegetation changes in the conservation management of forests (1992).
112 Creating new native woodlands (1994).
123 Managing rides, roadsides and edge habitats in lowland forests (2001).
124 An Ecological Site Classification for forestry in Great Britain (2001).
125 Climate change: impacts on UK forests (2002).

### Information Notes
15 Creating new native woodlands: turning ideas into reality (1999).
23 Using natural colonisation to create or expand new woodlands (1999).
28 Domestic stock grazing to enhance woodland biodiversity (1999).
32 Plant communities and soil seedbanks in broadleaved–conifer mixtures on ancient woodland sites in lowland Britain (2000).
35 Natural regeneration in broadleaved woodlands: deer browsing and the establishment of advance regeneration (2000).

36 The impact of deer on woodland biodiversity (2000).

**Handbooks**
Lichens in southern woodlands (1989).
Forestry practice (1991).
Tree shelters (1991).
Growing broadleaves for timber (1993).

**Field Book**
The use of herbicides in the forest (3rd edition) (1994).

**Woodland Grant Scheme**
Applicants' pack (2002).
(www.forestry.gov.uk)

**Scottish Forestry Grants Scheme**
Applicants' Booklet (2003).
(www.forestry.gov.uk/scotland)

For further information and details of new Forestry Commission publications visit:
**www.forestry.gov.uk/publications**
Electronic (pdf) versions of many titles are available to download.

## Other publications

ANDERSON, M.L. (1967). *A history of Scottish forestry*. Nelson, London.

ANON. (1995). Biodiversity: the UK Steering Group report. Volume 2: *Action Plans*. HMSO, London.

BUCKLEY, G.P. (Ed) (1992). *Ecology and management of coppice woodlands*. Chapman and Hall, London.

ENGLISH NATURE (1998). UK Biodiversity Group Tranche 2 Action Plans. Volume II: *terrestrial and freshwater habitats*. English Nature, Peterborough.

HALL, J.E. and KIRBY, K.J. (1998). *The relationship between biodiversity action plan priority and broad woodland habitat types, and other woodland classifications*. JNCC Report No. 288. Joint Nature Conservation Committee, Peterborough.

HARDING, P.T. and ROSE, F. (1986). *Pasture woodlands in lowland Britain*. Institute of Terrestrial Ecology, Monk's Wood, Huntingdon.

KIRBY, K.J. (1988). *A woodland survey handbook*. Research and Survey in Nature Conservation No 11. Nature Conservancy Council/Joint Nature Conservation Consultative Committee, Peterborough.

KIRBY, K.J., PETERKEN, G.F., SPENCER, J.W. and WALKER, G.J. (1989) (2nd edition). *Inventories of ancient semi-natural woodland* (Focus on Nature Conservation No 6). Nature Conservancy Council/Joint Nature Conservation Consultative Committee, Peterborough.

KIRBY, K.J. and SPENCER, J.W. (1992). An inventory of ancient woodland for England and Wales. In: *Biological Conservation* **62**, 77–93.

LINNARD, W. (1982). *Welsh woods and forests: history and utilisation*. National Museum of Wales.

MARREN, P. (1992). *The wild woods*. A regional guide to Britain's ancient woodland. David and Charles, London.

PRESTON, C.D., PEARMAN, D.A. and DINES, T.D. (2002). *New atlas of the British and Irish flora*. Oxford University Press, Oxford.

RACKHAM, O. (1980). *Ancient woodland: its history, vegetation and uses in England*. Edward and Arnold, London.

ROBERTS, A.J., RUSSELL, C., WALKER, G.J. and KIRBY, K.J. (1992). Regional variation in the origin, extent and composition of Scottish woodland. In: *Botanical Journal of Scotland* **46** (2), 167–189.

THE WOODLAND LEAD COORDINATION NETWORK FOR THE JOINT NATURE CONSERVATION COMMITTEE (2002). *Objective setting and condition monitoring within woodland Sites of Special Scientific Interest*. English Nature Research Report 472. English Nature, Peterborough.

VERA, F.W.M. (2000). *Grazing ecology and forest history*. CABI Publishing, Oxon.

WALKER, G.J. and KIRBY, K.J. (1989). *Inventories of ancient long-established and semi-natural woodland for Scotland*. Nature Conservancy Council.

WATKINS, C. (1990). *Britain's ancient woodland. Woodland management and conservation*. David and Charles, London.

WHITBREAD, A. M. and KIRBY K. J. (1992). *Summary of National Vegetation Classification woodland descriptions*. UK Nature Conservation No. 4. Joint Nature Conservation Committee, Peterborough.

# Appendix

# Definitions and classification of ancient and semi-natural woodlands

## Definitions

### Ancient woods

Ancient woods are those occupying sites which have been wooded continuously for several hundred years at least since the time when the first reliable maps were made. In England and Wales ancient woods are those known to have been present by around 1600 AD. In Scotland ancient woods are those which were present before 1750 when the first national survey was made by General Roy.

In both cases the dates correspond roughly with the time when new woodland planting first became commonplace so that ancient woods are unlikely to have been planted originally.

Some may be remnants of our prehistoric woodland (primary woods) whilst others arose as secondary woodland on ground cleared at some time in the past.

An ancient woodland may be over 400 years old but this does not mean that the present trees are as old as that, although in some woods this is the case; rather that woodland has been present on the site continuously without intervening periods under other land-uses.

In fact many ancient woods have been cut down and regrown (or been replanted) several times in recent centuries, and during this century many have been converted from native species to plantations of introduced trees.

**Figure 1** Classification of woodlands according to age and naturalness

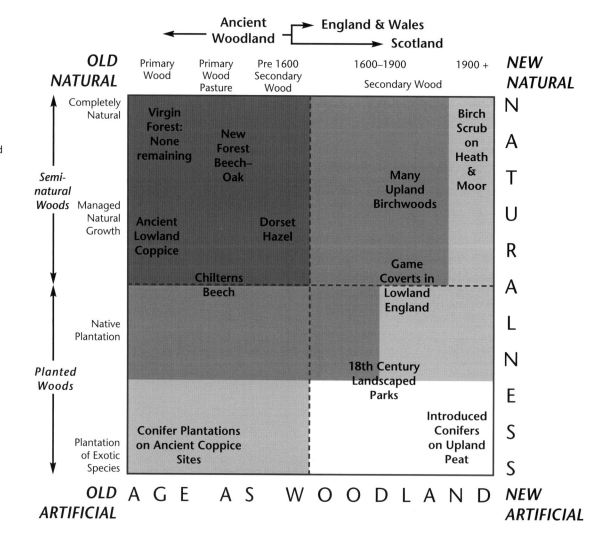

## Semi-natural woods

Semi-natural woods are stands which are composed predominantly of native trees and shrub species which have not been planted. By 'native' we mean locally native, e.g. beech is not native in Scotland and Scots pine is not native in England. Many woods are semi-natural even though they contain a few planted trees, for the latter do not change the character of the wood. The problem lies with woods dominated by native trees which were planted long ago on sites where they grew naturally, such as the many beech woods on the southern chalklands. Another ambiguous type is the chestnut coppice, dominated by an introduced species, often planted about 1800, but containing an admixture of native broadleaves and managed by the traditional coppice system. Both these 'intermediate' types are usually classified as 'semi-natural' by ecologists.

'Ancient' and 'semi-natural' have sometimes been used as synonyms, but this is quite wrong. Ancientness refers to the site as woodland, whereas naturalness refers to what is growing on that site.

## Combining ancient with semi-natural

The age of the site as woodland and the naturalness of the stand on a site are independent of each other. This is illustrated in Figure 1. The vertical axis of the diagram shows a range of naturalness from completely natural at the top (i.e. people have had no influence on its composition) to completely artificial at the bottom. The horizontal axis shows a range of age-as-woodland, from primary woods on the left (i.e. surviving remnants of prehistoric woodland which have never been completely cleared) to woods of very recent origin on the right.

Ancient woods are simply those in the left-hand half of the diagram: those in the right-hand half are recent woods (except in Scotland where ancient woods extend further to the right). Recent woods are often called secondary woods, but this is slightly inaccurate, for there are secondary woods originating in the Middle Ages or earlier, which are included with the ancient woods. Semi-natural woods are those in the upper half of the diagram. Those in the lower half are planted woods. Ancient, semi-natural woods are those in the top-left quarter.

Within the diagram various examples of woodland types are placed according to their degrees of ancientness and naturalness. Top left would be virgin forest, if it still existed in Britain. At the other extreme, bottom right, is the most artificial form of recent woodland, a conifer plantation on drained peat in the uplands. Such forest comprises an introduced species, planted in regular formation on sites modified by management, where trees may not have grown naturally for several millennia. In the other corners are two kinds of intermediate condition. In the top right corner, newly and naturally-regenerated birch scrub on heaths or moors exemplifies woods which are relatively natural, but which are extremely recent in origin. In the bottom left corner is a conifer plantation, often for Norway spruce or Corsican pine, growing in a wood which had been treated as coppice continuously for several centuries. This is a common condition in lowland England: the site has been woodland continuously for a millennium or more, but the stand is almost wholly artificial. The diagram also shows roughly where several other woodland types fit.

## Ancient semi-natural woods

Figure 1 makes clear that ASNW as a class contains many types of woodland. Some are very ancient, but others originated in historic times. Some are much more natural than others. Borderline types exist, and for different reasons.

Ancient semi-natural woods, because of their combination of naturalness and a long continuous history, are generally richer for wildlife and support more rare habitats and species than more recent or less natural woods.

However, all these divisions are somewhat arbitrary points on a spectrum and mature 'recent' semi-natural woods and old plantations of native species can also develop a high ecological value and of course landscape value, which may justify similar management to that of ancient semi-natural woods as Figure 1 indicates. This is particularly the case in the uplands where in general the ecological differences between ancient and younger woods are less marked than in lowland areas.

Inventories of ancient and semi-natural woodland were prepared by the former Nature

Conservancy Council (NCC) from map and historical records and some survey information.

Owners can refer to these to check the status of their woods either by consulting the NCC's successor bodies (English Nature, Scottish Natural Heritage and Countryside Council for Wales) or local Forestry Authority offices each of which holds copies of the inventory.

## Classification of ancient semi-natural woodlands

### Outline

For the purposes of these management guides, Britain's ancient semi-natural woodlands have been divided into 8 types. This gives the best balance between straight-forward, practical guidance and the specific needs of the various types of native woodland. Many more types are recognisable, but fine distinctions would over-complicate the advice. With fewer types important ecological and silvicultural distinctions would be lost.

The 8 woodland types are based on 4 major regional divisions of Britain shown approximately in Figure 2:

- The uplands of the north and west (Upland zone);

- The 'boreal' region of the Scottish Highlands within the Upland zone, in which pine is native (Pine zone);

- The lowlands of the south and east (Lowland zone);

- The southern districts of the lowlands within the natural range of beech (Beech zone).

**Figure 2**  The main semi-natural woodland zones

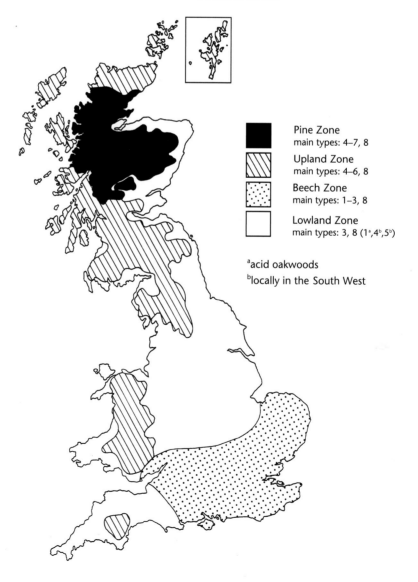

**Pine Zone**
main types: 4–7, 8

**Upland Zone**
main types: 4–6, 8

**Beech Zone**
main types: 1–3, 8

**Lowland Zone**
main types: 3, 8 (1$^a$,4$^b$,5$^b$)

$^a$acid oakwoods
$^b$locally in the South West

These geographical divisions are further divided to recognise the ecological differences between acid and base-poor soils on the one hand and alkaline and base-rich soils on the other. Wetland woods constitute an additional type found in all regions.

The result is 8 types whose main characteristics are summarised below and in Table 1. They can be related to existing classifications, particularly the National Vegetation Classification (Rodwell 1991[1]) and the stand types described by Peterken (1981[6]). Insofar as the complexities of native woodlands can be reflected in a simple scheme, each type has a distinctive ecological and regional character, different history of management and exploitation, and different management requirements in the future. The guides have been drawn up for typical examples of each type.

The classification helps to relate British woodlands to those of continental Europe. The boreal pine and birch woods form an outlier of the sub-arctic coniferous forests. The

beechwoods are the extremity of the central European broadleaved woods. Upland broadleaved woods have their counterpart in the oceanic woods of Ireland, Brittany and Galicia. The lowland mixed broadleaved woods form an outlier of a zone of mixed woodland lacking beech which extends throughout central Europe and deep into Asia.

## Descriptions of each type

### Lowland acid beech and oak woods
NVC types W15, W16
Stand types 6C, 6D, 8A, 8B

Beech and oak woods on acid, generally light soils. South-eastern, mainly in Weald, London and Hampshire basins. Mostly treated as high forest or wood-pasture in the immediate past. Many had a more distant history of coppicing, and in the Chilterns and the south-east some still have this character. Many were planted with chestnut around 1800 and are still worked as coppice. Includes a scatter of strongly acid

**Table 1**    Summary of the main ecological and silvicultural characteristics of the eight semi-natural woodland types

| Semi-natural woodland type | Ecological characteristics | | Silvicultural characteristics | |
|---|---|---|---|---|
| | NVC communities | Peterken stand types | Main historic management | Emphasis in future management |
| **South and East Britain** | | | | |
| 1. Lowland acid beech and oak woods* | W15, W16 | 6C, 6D, 8A, 8B | C or WP | HF |
| 2. Lowland beech–ash woods* | W12, W13, W14 | [1A], [3C], 8C, 8D, 8E | C or HF | HF |
| 3. Lowland mixed broadleaved woods | W8 (A–D), W10 | 1B, 2A, 2B, 2C, 3A, 3B, 4A, 4B, 4C, 5A, 5B, 7C, 9A, 9B, 10A, 10B | C | C or HF |
| **North and West Britain** | | | | |
| 4. Upland mixed ashwoods | W8 (E–G), W9 | 1A, 1C, 1D, 3C, 3D, 7D, [8A–E] | C or HF | HF(C) |
| 5. Upland oakwoods | W11, W17 (Oak dominant) | 6A, 6B, [8A–B] | C or HF grazed | HF(grazed) |
| 6. Upland birchwoods | W11, W17 (Birch dominant) | 12A–B | HF grazed | HF(grazed) |
| 7. Native pinewoods** | W18, W19 | 11A–C | HF grazed | HF(grazed) |
| **All regions** | | | | |
| 8. Wet woodlands | W1, W2, W3, W4, W5, W6, W7 | 7A–B, 7E | C neglect | Minimum intervention |

NVC: National Vegetation Classification  C: Coppice  WP: Wood Pasture  HF: High Forest
*Restricted to zone where beech is native (SE Wales and S England)  **Restricted to zone of native pine (Scottish Highlands)

oak-dominated coppices found throughout the English lowlands. Also includes associated birch woods, self-sown Scots pine woods, holly scrub. Enclaves of hornbeam on acid soils best regarded as part of this type.

### Lowland beech–ash woods
NVC types W12, W13, W14
Stand types 8C, 8D, 8E and parts of 1C, 3C

Beech woods on heavy and/or alkaline soils and associated ash woods. Southern distribution, grouped in South Downs, North Downs, Chilterns, Cotswold scarp, Lower Wye Valley and south Wales limestones, but sparingly elsewhere. Most had a medieval history of coppicing with limited wood-pasture, but most have long since been converted to high forest, often with extreme dominance of beech. Coppice survives in western districts. Woods often on steep slopes, but they extend on to Chiltern and Downland plateaux. Associated ash woods usually mark sites of past disturbance or formerly unwooded ground. Yew common in the driest beech woods and as distinct yew woods on open downland.

### Lowland mixed broadleaved woods
NVC types W8(a–d), W10
Stand types 1B, 2A, 2B, 2C, 3A, 3B, 4A, 4B, 4C, 5A, 7C, 9A, 10A and 10B

Often known as 'oak–ash woods' by past ecologists, these are largely dominated by mixtures of oak, ash and hazel, but other trees may be dominant, notably lime (4A, 4B, 5A and 5B), hornbeam (9A and 9B), suckering elms (10A), wych elm (1B), field maple (2A, 2B and 2C) and alder (7C). Occur throughout the lowlands and upland margins, with enclaves on fertile soils in SW Wales, NE Wales and E Scotland. Most treated as coppice until 20th century, some still worked. Many still have a stock of oak standards growing with a mixture of other species grown from coppice and seedling regeneration. The various stand types occur as intricate mosaics which present silvicultural problems. Many have been invaded by sycamore or chestnut. Disturbed ground often marked by abundant ash, hawthorn or birch.

### Upland mixed ashwoods
NVC types W8(e–g), W9
Stand types 1A, 1C, 1D, 3C, 3D, 7D with 8A–E where beech has been introduced.

Dominated by ash, wych elm and/or oak, usually with hazel underwood, sometimes with scattered gean. Found throughout the uplands on limestone and other base-rich sites. Also characteristic of lower slopes and flushed sites within upland oak woods. In the very oceanic climate of the north and west, increasingly take the form of ash–hazel woods with birch and rowan containing lower slopes dominated by alder. Lime is regular and sometimes common north to the Lake District. Like other upland woods, many have a history of coppicing which was displaced by grazing. Sycamore is a common colonist and in many woods is a naturalised part of the mixture.

### Upland oakwoods
NVC types W11, W17 (oak-dominated woods)
Stand types 6A, 6B with 8A, 8B where beech has been introduced.

Woods dominated by sessile oak and, less often, pedunculate oak, growing on base-poor, often thin soils in upland districts from Sutherland to Cornwall. Sometimes absolutely dominated by oak, but more often oak forms mixtures with birch and rowan on very acid soils and hazel on the more fertile sites. Oak was planted in many woods, even those which now seem remote. Coppicing was characteristic, but not prevalent in N Wales and NW Scotland. Most now neglected and heavily grazed by sheep and deer. Includes small enclaves of birch, ash, holly, hawthorn and rowan-dominated woodland.

### Upland birchwoods
NVC types W11, W17(birch-dominated woods)
Stand types 12A, 12B

Woods dominated by birch, but sometimes containing many hazel, sallow, rowan and holly. Birchwoods occur throughout Britain. Some are secondary woods which can sometimes develop naturally into native pinewoods or upland oakwoods. This type covers 'Highland Birchwoods' together with the extensive birchwoods of upland England and

Wales. Most are now heavily grazed by sheep and deer. Lowland birch stands are usually temporary phases or small enclaves and are included in Types 1 and 3.

## Native pinewoods
NVC types W18, W19
Stand types 11A, 11B, 11C

Scots pine-dominated woods and the associated enclaves of birch and other broadleaves in the Highlands. Tend to be composed mainly of older trees, with natural regeneration often scarce. Most subjected to exploitive fellings during the last 400 years and heavy deer grazing during the last century.

## Wet woodlands
NVC types W1, W2, W3, W4, W5, W6 and W7
Stand types 7A, 7B and 7E

Woodland and scrub on wet soils and flood plains. Usually dominated by alder, willow or birch. Generally take the form of scrub or coppice. Fragments of the prehistoric flood plain woods of black poplar, pedunculate oak, ash, elm, alder tree willows, and occasional black poplar survive in some southern districts.

# Problems in using the classification

Semi-natural woodlands are complex systems which throw up many problems in the construction and use of classifications. These may seem unwelcome to managers used to managing plantations of one or two species, with clearly defined stand boundaries, but management of complexity is unavoidable if the small-scale diversity of semi-natural woodlands is to be successfully conserved. The commonest problems and their solutions are:

## Intermediates
Stands falling between two or more types. Examples include;

- **a sessile oakwood on the Welsh borderland (between types 1 and 5);**

- **a mixed woodland with a limited amount of beech (between types 1 or 2 and 3–5);**

- **a birch-rich pinewood (between types 6–7);**

- **Managers should use the Guides appropriate to both types.**

## Mosaics
Woodlands may include more than one of the 8 types within their border. Example: lowland acid beech woods and upland oak woods commonly include patches of birch-wood.

Ideally, each patch should be treated separately, though this is impractical with small inclusions of less than 0.5 ha.

## Outliers
Good examples of each type can occur outwith their region. Examples: good lowland mixed broadleaved woods occasionally occur in N Wales and SW Wales; birchwoods occur throughout the lowlands.

Management of outlying examples should be based on the guidance for their core regions, but some adaptation may be required for local circumstances.

## Introductions
Semi-natural woods often contain trees growing beyond their native range. Common examples are beech in northern England, north Wales and Scotland, and Scots pine south of the Highlands.

Unless the introduced species is dominant, such woods should be treated in the same way as the original type, using the guidance given on introduced species within that type. Thus, for example, a beech wood on acid soils in the Lake District should be treated as an acid beech wood (type 1) if beech is dominant, but otherwise should be treated as an upland oakwood (type 5).

# Notes